THE ELOISE WILKIN TREASURY

Favorite Nursery Rhymes, Prayers, Poems, and Stories
illustrated by Eloise Wilkin

THE ELOISE WILKIN TREASURY

Favorite Nursery Rhymes, Prayers, Poems, and Stories
illustrated by Eloise Wilkin

edited by Linda C. Falken

A GOLDEN BOOK • NEW YORK
Western Publishing Company, Inc., Racine, Wisconsin 53404

This book is affectionately dedicated
to my husband, Sid,
and to our four children,
Ann, Sidney, Debra, and Jeremy

—E.W.

Table of Contents

The year's at the spring
And day's at the morn;
Morning's at seven;
The hillside's dew-pearled;
The lark's on the wing;
The snail's on the thorn:
God's in his heaven—
All's right with the world.

—*Robert Browning*
from Pippa Passes

6

…What is Spring?—
Growth in every thing—

Flesh and fleece, fur and feather,
Grass and greenworld all together;
Star-eyed strawberry-breasted
Throstle above her nested

Cluster of bugle blue eggs thin
Forms and warms the life within;
And bird and blossom swell
In sod or sheath or shell.

—*Gerard Manley Hopkins*
from The May Magnificat

ll About Babies

A baby is soft, a baby is small.
A baby is special.
Baby's clothes are soft and small—
just right for a baby.

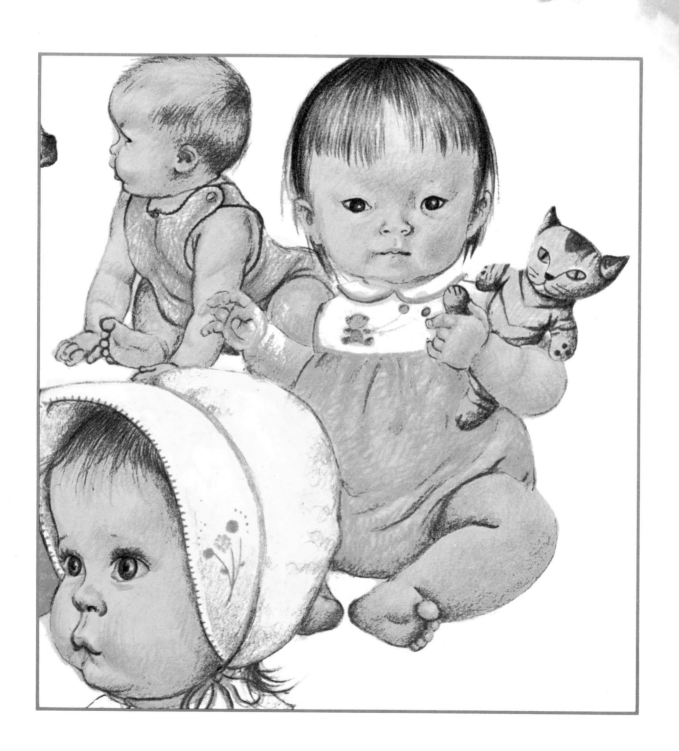

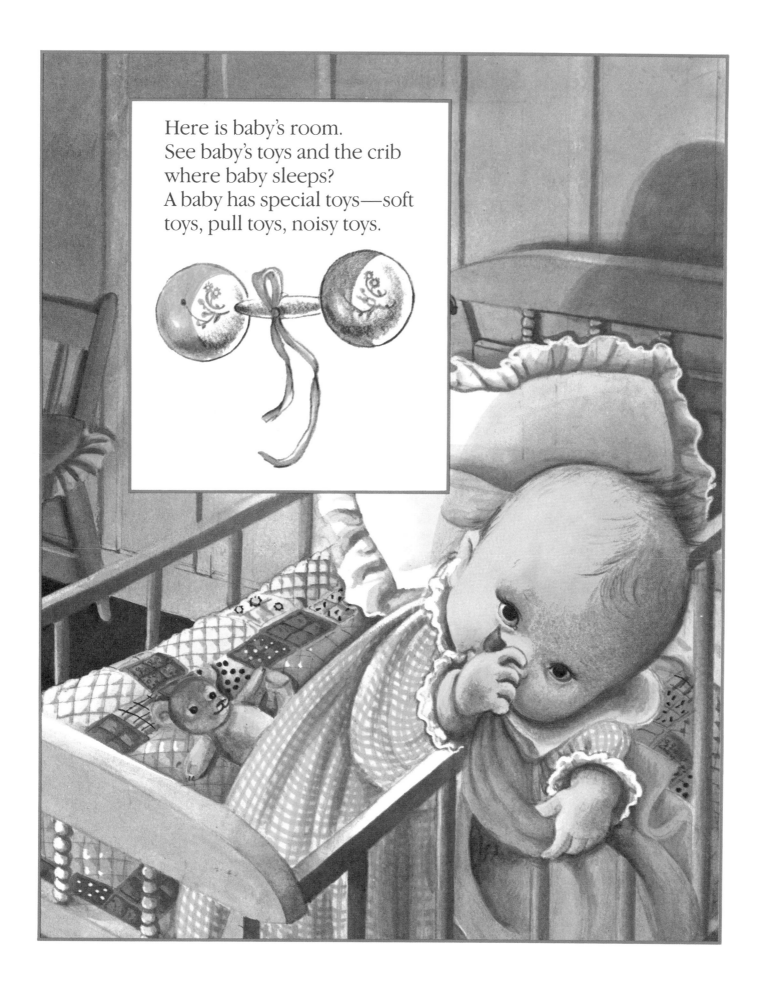

Here is baby's room.
See baby's toys and the crib
where baby sleeps?
A baby has special toys—soft
toys, pull toys, noisy toys.

Baby plays with a ball.
See baby smile?
Can you see her baby teeth?

Splash! Baby likes to play in the tub.

10

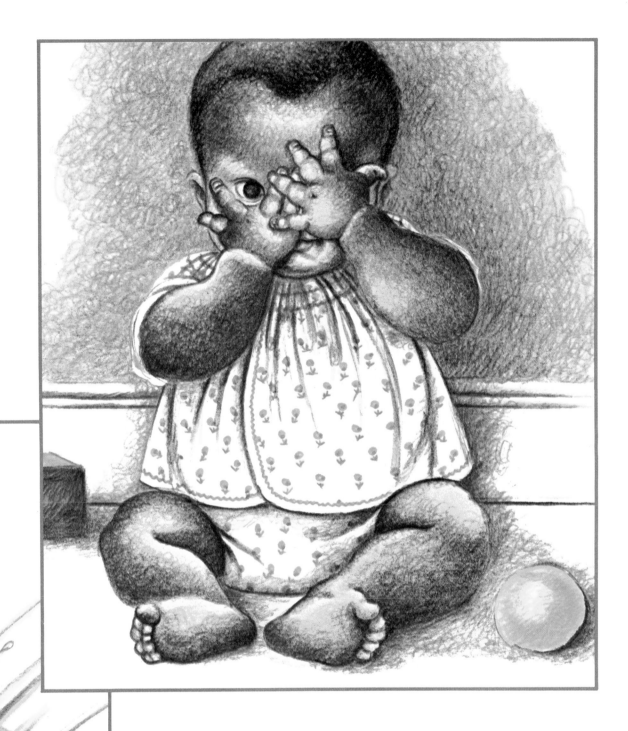

Peek-a-boo! I see you!
Baby loves this game.

11

Mother holds baby while he drinks.
It is a happy time for both of them.

A baby gets sleepy.
Good night, baby.

Sippity Sup, Sippity Sup

Sippity sup, sippity sup,
Bread and milk from a china cup,
Bread and milk from a bright silver spoon,
Made of a piece of the bright silver moon!
Sippity sup, sippity sup,
Sippity, sippity sup!

Pat-a-Cake

Pat-a-cake, pat-a-cake,
    baker's man!
Bake me a cake
    as fast as you can;
Roll it and pat it
    and mark it with "B,"
And put it in the oven
    for baby and me.

Baby Looks and Baby Listens

What are some things that baby sees
besides his own small hands and knees?

He sees a beetle on the ground,
crawling round and round and round.

He sees buttercups and purple clover,
leans down to sniff—oops!—tumbles over.

Look! It's started raining and baby's gone inside.
The thunder doesn't scare him.
He isn't one to hide.

He sees how dark the clouds are, still he doesn't cry.
He smiles at the rainbow shining in the sky.

What are some sounds that baby hears
when she listens with her little ears?

Tick-tock, tick-tock—
that's the sound of baby's clock.

Tum-tum, tum-dee-dum—
Baby's beating on her drum.

The Birthday Party

Daddy's very busy

…and sister is, too

…and Mommy and big brother

…why all this to-do?

21

Surprise! It's baby's birthday,
and there will be such fun
when we sing the birthday song
to baby, who's turned one.

Now we'll blow the candle out.
See that baby smile?

It's fun to open presents
and play with them awhile!

Happy Birthday!

Little Boy Blue

Little Boy Blue,
  come blow your horn!
The sheep's in the meadow,
  the cow's in the corn.
Where's the boy
  that looks after the sheep?
He's under the haycock,
  fast asleep.

Where Did the Baby Go?

One day, a curious little girl saw something lying on a table. When she picked it up, she saw a picture of a baby—a round, happy-looking baby wearing a big, floppy hat.

She ran to show her mother what she had found.

"Who is it?" the little girl asked.

"Can't you guess?" replied her mother.

"No," said the little girl. "Have I ever seen this baby?"

"Yes. In a way, you used to see her every single day."

The little girl thought very hard. "Where did the baby go?" she asked.

"Well," said her mother, "when she first lived here, she didn't go anywhere at all. She spent most of the day sleeping."

The little girl was quiet for a moment. Then she jumped up and ran into her room. She looked in her new pink and white bed. There was no baby.

She looked in her mother and father's big blue bed. But there was no baby.

She looked in the corner of the kitchen where Duke slept on a cushion. But there was no baby. Where did the baby go?

"I can't find her," the little girl said when she came back to her mother.

"Oh, she stopped being a sleepyhead quite a while ago," said her mother. "Soon after, she began to crawl all over the house, like a brand-new puppy."

"Then I'll just go where Duke used to go when he was a puppy!" said the little girl.

She crawled behind the couch, and there she found three shiny pennies! But there was no baby.

She crawled under the dining room table, and there she found Duke's rubber bone. But there was no baby. Where did the baby go?

"I still can't find her," the little girl said.

"Are you sure?" asked her mother. "She doesn't crawl around like a puppy anymore. Now she likes to play games."

"Games!" cried the little girl. "What kind of games?"

"One of her favorites is hide-and-seek," said her mother.

"That's one of MY favorites! I'll go and look in all the good hiding places."

She looked in the hall closet, and out tumbled Daddy's snow boots. But there was no baby.

She looked behind the living room curtains, and there was her yellow teddy bear. But there was no baby. Where did the baby go?

"That baby isn't anywhere," the little girl said to her mother.

"I think that if you'll look one more time, you'll find her," her mother said. "I'll give you one more hint: she likes to dress up in my clothes."

The little girl ran off to her mother's closet and flung open the door.

She searched among the dresses. But there was no baby.

She searched among the shoes. But there was no baby.

She searched among the hats, and there was the hat that baby was wearing in the picture!

The little girl sat on the floor in front of the mirror and tried on the hat. She turned this way and that to see how she looked.

Suddenly she looked closer at the face peering out at her from under the hat.

"My eyes are blue—just like that baby's," she said to herself.
"And my nose looks just like that baby's, too—only bigger. I
even smile like that baby. I LOOK JUST LIKE THAT BABY," she
said out loud, "ONLY I'M BIGGER!"

Running back to her mother, the little girl called out,
"Mommy, I know where the baby went!"

"You do?" said her mother, looking all around the room.
"Where is she?"

"Here I am!" the little girl said. "Right in front of you!"

Little Lamb, who made thee?
  Dost thou know who made thee?
Gave thee life and bid thee feed,
By the stream and o'er the mead;
Gave thee clothing of delight,
Softest clothing, wooly, bright;
Gave thee such a tender voice,
Making all the vales rejoice?
  Little Lamb, who made thee?
  Dost thou know who made thee?

—William Blake
from The Lamb

[T]he New Baby

One day, a big green truck stopped in front of Mike's house. The deliveryman took a large box from the truck and carried it to the porch, where Mike was playing.

"Hello," Mike said to the deliveryman.

The deliveryman said, "Hello, there."

"Is that for us?" asked Mike.

"Yes," said the deliveryman.

"What's in it?" asked Mike.

"It's a buggy," the deliveryman said. He rang the doorbell.

Mike's mommy came to the door. "Bring the box right in," she said.

The deliveryman put the box by the window and left.

"What's a buggy, Mommy?" Mike asked.

Before Mommy could answer, Daddy came in. "Aha!" he said. "Here's our new buggy."

"What *is* a buggy?" asked Mike again.

"It's a little bed on wheels," said Daddy. "You've seen them lots of times. It's for the new baby."

"Whose baby?" Mike asked.

"Our baby," Daddy said. "Before long, we're going to have a new baby."

"We are?" Mike said. "What will it be like? Will it be a little girl? Will it be a boy? When is it coming?"

"Hold on a minute!" said Daddy, laughing. "We don't know yet. It will be a surprise."

A few days later, Aunt Pat came to visit. "She's going to help us take care of the baby," said Daddy.

At supper, Mike asked, "Who will bring the baby?"

"No one will," said Mommy. "I'll go to the hospital soon, and the baby will be born there."

That night Mike woke up while it was still dark. Aunt Pat and Daddy were in the hallway. Mommy stood by Mike's bed with her coat on.

"Where are you going?" Mike asked.

Mommy kissed Mike and smiled. "I'm going to the hospital to have our baby," she said. "I'll bring it home very soon."

In the morning, Mike helped Aunt Pat set the table. Then he ate every bit of his breakfast.

The telephone rang. Mike got there first. It was Daddy calling.

Daddy said, "Mike, you have a beautiful baby sister!"

"Aunt Pat, I have a sister!" Mike said as he handed the telephone to Aunt Pat.

Before long, Daddy came home.

"Where's Mommy and the baby?" asked Mike.

"They'll be home soon," said Daddy.

But it seemed like a very long time that Mike had to wait. Daddy went to see Mommy and the baby, and so did Aunt Pat. Mike wanted to go, too, but he was still too little to visit in the hospital.

Mike and Daddy talked about the baby's name. Daddy said, "Mommy suggested naming her Pat, after Aunt Pat."

"I like that," said Mike.

"So do I," said Daddy.

So it was decided.

"When will Mommy bring her home?" Mike asked.

"Tomorrow," said Daddy.

The next day, Daddy went to drive Mommy and little Pat home from the hospital. Mike sat on the steps and waited. At last a blue car turned the corner. It was Mike's car.

"Hello, Mike!" Mommy called. "We're home!"

Mike ran down the sidewalk to the car. Daddy got out first, then Mommy and little Pat. Mommy handed the baby to Daddy, and gave Mike a big kiss and a hug. "It's so good to be home again," she said.

Mike looked at the baby. She had tiny hands and blue eyes. Her hair was soft and wispy. After they went inside, Mike asked, "May I hold our baby?"

"Of course you may," Mommy said.

Mike sat on the couch. He sat way back and held the baby just right. How proud Mike was! It's wonderful to have a new baby, he thought.

The sea! the sea! the open sea!
The blue, the fresh, the ever free!
Without a mark, without a bound,
It runneth the earth's wide region round,
It plays with the clouds; it mocks the skies,
Or like a cradled creature lies.

—*Barry Cornwall*

Great, wide, beautiful, wonderful World,
With the wonderful water round you curled,
And the wonderful grass upon your breast,
World, you are beautifully dressed.

—*W. B. Rands*
from Wonderful World

38

Bring back the singing; and the scent
   Of meadowlands at dewy prime;—
Oh, bring again my heart's content,
   Thou Spirit of the Summertime!

—*William Allingham*

39

The Boy With a Drum

There once was a boy
With a little toy drum—
Rat-a-tat-tat-a-tat
Rum-a-tum-tum.

One day he went marching
And played on his drum—

Rat-a-tat-tat-a-tat
Rum-a-tum-tum.

Soon he was joined
By a friendly old cat—
Rum-a-tum-tum-a-tum
Rat-a-tat-tat.

Next they were joined
By a green spotted frog
Who sat by the road
On an old brown log.

And then they were joined
By a big yellow dog
Who marched down the road
With the green spotted frog.

They marched by a field,
They marched by a house—
And were joined by a cow
And a furry brown mouse.

They marched by a horse
Who was pulling a plow,
And he trotted behind them
And followed the cow.

Next they were joined by a big
    white duck
And an old mother chicken
With a cluck-cluck-cluck.

And a pig and a goose
And a billy goat, too,
And a big red rooster
With a cock-a-doodle-doo.

And they all went marching
With a rat-a-tat-tat,
The boy with his drum
And the big friendly cat.

The horse and the cow
And the mouse and the dog,
The duck and the chicken
And the pig and the frog.

The goose and the rooster
And the billy goat, too,
With a baa, honk, quack,
And a cock-a-doodle-doo,

Oink, bow-wow, and a
Moo-moo-moo,
Neigh, cluck, squeak,
And a mew-mew-mew.

They all marched away
To the top of a hill—
If they haven't stopped marching,
They'll be marching still.

Clouds

White sheep, white sheep,
On a blue hill,
When the wind stops
You all stand still.
When the wind blows
You walk away slow.
White sheep, white sheep,
Where do you go?

—*Christina Rossetti*

44

Wiggles

One day Donnie went with his mother to see Mrs. Jones. Mrs. Jones lived on a farm. Donnie had never been there before.

Mrs. Jones said, "I'm so glad to meet you, Donnie. Go hunt around outdoors and find Wiggles to play with you."

Donnie didn't know who Wiggles was. He could have asked Mrs. Jones but he didn't like to. He went out to look around.

Donnie walked past the barn. There in a pen were five little piglets with their mother. The piglets poked and nosed and wiggled their little curly tails.

Could one of these little pigs be Wiggles? wondered Donnie.

"Have these little pigs got names?" Donnie asked an old man sitting nearby on a chopping block.

"Not yet," the old man said.

Donnie walked on along a lane and wondered and wondered.

Could Wiggles be one of the butterflies hovering over the clover?

Could Wiggles be one of the little chickens pecking, pecking?

Could the old mother hen be Wiggles?

Or the rooster strutting around with his handsome tail?

But how could you play with butterflies, or little chicks that ran so fast, or a mother hen who squawked and fluttered away, or that big rooster looking so proud and fierce?

Donnie walked on. A baby calf with wobbly legs was standing by its mother in a field. A man stood there, stroking the little calf's neck.

"Has that little calf got a name?" Donnie called to the man.

"My wife just calls him Pet," the man shouted back. "Why don't you go find Wiggles? Look in the orchard."

Donnie wanted to ask him who Wiggles was, but he was afraid it might sound silly. He walked toward the orchard.

There was a curly-haired dog sniffing the ground, sniff-sniff-sniff.

Could this be Wiggles? wondered Donnie. All the dogs he knew had names. This one's name might be Wiggles.

A little old woman hobbled out of the orchard.

Donnie asked her, "What is that dog's name, please?"

"His name's Jip," the old woman said. "Why don't you go find Wiggles? Last tree down this row. Come, Jip." She hobbled away. Jip trotted after her.

Donnie walked along the row of trees until he came to the last one. There was a ladder leaning against it.

"Hi!" said a voice up among the branches. "Want to come up in my tree house?"

Donnie looked up and saw a boy looking down through the leaves.

"My name's Donnie. What's yours?" he asked. He put one foot on the ladder.

"Wiggles," the boy replied. "Did you ever have a tree house?"

"No," said Donnie. He climbed another step. "Why do they call you Wiggles?" he asked.

"Because I can wiggle my ears," Wiggles said. "Want to see?"

"Yes," said Donnie. "Can you show me how?"

"Sure. Come on up." Wiggles said.

So Donnie climbed up into the tree house, and Wiggles showed him. After that Donnie and Wiggles became good friends, and whenever Donnie came with his mother to visit Mrs. Jones, they played together.

I love all that thou lovest,
    Spirit of Delight:
The fresh Earth in new leaves dressed,
    and the starry night;
Autumn evening, and the morn
When the golden mists are born.

—Percy Bysshe Shelley
from Song

50

We Like Playschool

My name is Carol. I go to playschool
every day.

At playschool, Ms. Hall is our teacher.
She plays the piano. We sing, "Good
morning to you."

Michael feeds our fish. Susan feeds
our turtles. We take turns. Tomorrow
it will be my turn to feed the turtles.

We do finger painting.
I like to paint with blue.
Karen likes to paint with red.

We make animals out of clay.
I am making a dog. Douglas is
making an elephant.

We play games. We play "The Farmer in the Dell."

We listen quietly while Ms. Hall tells us stories. We like to hear stories.

We show and tell about things that happen. Mark told about his new baby sister. Eric showed us his pet hamster.

We have milk to drink. Jackie did not drink all of his milk.
We rest on our rugs. My rug is blue. Kim's rug is blue, too.
We go outside to play. I like to swing. We all take turns.

We draw pictures. Ms. Hall hangs our pictures on the wall. I drew a picture of my baby sister by our house.

Now it's time to go home.

"Goodbye, Ms. Hall. See you tomorrow."

At home I am the playschool teacher. I am Ms. Carol. My sister and Rusty and Patches are my boys and girls.

I play the piano. The children sing, "Good morning to you." Laurie sings loudly. She is glad to be in playschool.

Someone's loving, Lord.

Someone's praying, Lord.

Someone's giving, Lord.

Kumbaya

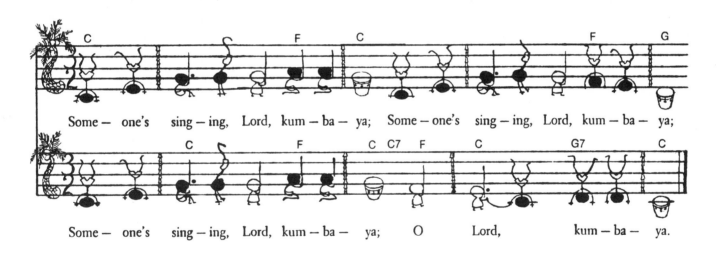

Some — one's sing — ing, Lord, kum — ba — ya; Some—one's sing — ing, Lord, kum — ba — ya;

Some — one's sing — ing, Lord, kum-ba — ya; O Lord, kum — ba — ya.

—Author Unknown

Someone's hungry, Lord

Someone's happy, Lord.

Someone's praising, Lord.

The Creation

In the beginning God created the heaven and the earth.

And the earth was without form and empty, and darkness was upon the face of the deep.

And God said, Let there be light. And there was light.

And God divided the light from the darkness.

And God called the light Day, and the darkness Night. And the evening and the morning were the first day.

And God said, Let there be space to divide the waters from the waters. And it was so.

And God called the space Heaven. And the evening and the morning were the second day.

And God said, Let the waters under the heaven be gathered together and let the dry land appear. And it was so.

And God called the dry land Earth; and the waters He called seas.

And God said, Let the earth bring forth grass, and herbs, and trees yielding fruit after its kind, whose seed is in itself. And it was so.

And the evening and the morning were the third day.

And God said, Let there be lights in the heaven to divide the day from the night; and let them be for seasons, and for days, and for years.

And God made two great lights; the greater light to rule the day, and the lesser light to rule the night. And He made the stars.

And the evening and the morning were the fourth day.

And God said, Let the waters bring forth fish that may swim in the sea, and birds that may fly above the earth in the heaven. And it was so.

And God blessed them, saying, Be fruitful, and multiply, and fill the waters in the seas, and let birds multiply on the earth.

And the evening and the morning were the fifth day.

And God said, Let the earth bring forth living creatures after their kind, cattle, and creeping things, and beasts of the earth. And it was so.

And God said, Let us make man in our image, after our likeness.

So God created man in His own image, male and female.

And God blessed them, and said unto them, Be fruitful and multiply.

And God saw every thing that He had made, and, behold it was very good. And the evening and the morning were the sixth day.

And on the seventh day God ended His work and He rested.

And God blessed the seventh day, because in it He had rested from all His work.

Georgie Finds a Grandpa

When Georgie was six he started going to first grade. He learned how to read. He learned how to print. And he learned how to add. But he also learned that other children had something he didn't have. Georgie didn't have a grandpa.

The boy who sat in front of Georgie had a grandpa who sent him oranges from Florida. The boy who sat beside him had a grandpa who could fix toys when they got broken. And Georgie's best friend was always bringing picture books to school—his grandpa had a book store.

Georgie began to think of all the different kinds of nice grandpas there must be. If you had a grandpa who worked in a book store, how about a grandpa who worked in a candy store? Or a soda fountain? Or a toy store? Or suppose you had a grandpa who was a farmer and would let you drive the tractor! Or a grandpa who was a clown and could make you laugh all day!

One day a new boy came to Georgie's class. He had two grandpas! A far-away grandpa who sent him letters and things— and a nearby grandpa who read stories to him at night.

Georgie didn't think it was fair that everybody had grandpas except him. He wanted a grandpa more than anything else in the world.

The next morning was Saturday. Georgie took his wallet that still had his birthday money in it and walked down the road. At the corner there was an antique shop. Mrs. McMath, the owner, saw Georgie and waved.

"Hi, there, where are you going so early?" she asked.

"On a trip," said Georgie. "I'm out hunting for something."

"Well, come here and get an apple to take along," said Mrs. McMath.

Georgie thought it would be a good idea to take an apple along in case he got hungry, so he went to the door of the shop.

"Georgie," said Mrs. McMath, as she gave him a nice red apple, "you've never been inside my shop. Wouldn't you like to see my antiques?"

"I don't know," said Georgie. "What are antiques, anyway?"

"Why, anything that is very old is an antique," she replied.

"In that case," said Georgie, "I'll come in and look around."

Georgie went into the shop. He saw a spinning wheel and a butter churn and a wooden cradle. He saw a lot of old lamps and chairs. But he didn't want any of them.

Then, at the back of the shop, he saw an old man sitting in a rocking chair. He had white hair and white eyebrows and nice blue eyes. He smiled at Georgie.

The old man was making a tiny ship with a mast and two sails. And when the ship was finished, he folded it together and before Georgie could say, "presto change-o," the ship was inside a bottle, sails and all.

Georgie walked back to Mrs. McMath.

"Well," she said, "did you see anything you liked?"

"Yes," said Georgie. "I'll take that." He pointed to the back of
the shop.

"You mean you want that old rocking chair?" asked Mrs. McMath.

"I mean I want that old grandpa," said Georgie. "I'll take him
home now."

"That's my father," said Mrs. McMath, "but you could have
him after school and on Saturdays."

"Today is Saturday," said Georgie, and he walked back to the
old man.

The old man was busy making another ship to fit inside a
bottle.

"That's a nice ship," said Georgie. "How come you make such good ships?"

"Well," said the old man, "I used to be a sea captain and sail all over the world."

"I'll bet you could tell a lot of good stories about ships and sailing," said Georgie.

"The only trouble is," the old man said, "I haven't got anybody to tell stories to."

"You have now," said Georgie, taking his hand.

On Monday morning the boy who sat in front of Georgie brought an orange from his grandpa's orange grove. The boy who sat beside him brought in a car that his grandpa had fixed. And Georgie's best friend brought in some picture books from his grandpa's store.

But Georgie brought in something new.

"Where did you get such a beautiful ship?" asked the teacher. "And how did it get inside that bottle?"

"My grandpa did it," said Georgie. "My grandpa can do lots of things!"

The North Wind

The north wind doth blow,
And we shall have snow,
And what will the robin do then,
    Poor thing?

He'll sit in the barn
And keep himself warm,
And hide his head under his wing,
    Poor thing!

Good Night

There was once a little girl who, strange as it may seem, did not like to go to bed.

Every evening she wanted to stay up and play.

Every evening her mother said, "Bedtime, dear! Hurry and get ready for bed."

And every evening that little girl replied, "But I am wide awake. I still want to play."

So one evening her mother said, "Very well, you may stay up. But I am afraid you will have to play by yourself."

"Your brothers are going to sleep, and your daddy and I are going to sleep, so you will be all alone. Good night, my little wide-awake girl."

"Good night," said the little girl. "I do not mind being alone. I will play with my toys."

First she went to her dollhouse.

But her dolls had been playing all day long, and now they were fast asleep.

"Well, then," said the little girl to herself, "I will build with the blocks."

So she looked for her blocks, but they were all tucked away for the night.

"Oh," she said. "Well, I will play with the Noah's Ark."

But the Noah's Ark was dark and silent.

All the animals two by two were fast asleep. Mr. and Mrs. Noah were fast asleep, too.

65

"Well," said the little girl, "I will play with my sleepy doll. She sleeps all day, so she must be wide awake at night."

But the sleepy doll was upstairs in the little girl's bedroom.

So the little girl crept very quietly up the stairs...

past the room where her brothers were fast asleep...

and past the room where her father and mother were fast asleep, and into her own little room.

There was the sleepy doll, fast asleep, too.

The little girl decided to sing to her, anyway. She sang her favorite song:

"Rock-a-bye, baby, on the treetop,
When the wind blows, the cradle will rock."

Everything was so dark and quiet and full of sleep that the little girl's eyes began to close.

So she took her sleepy doll in her arms and curled up in her own little bed, and soon that wide-awake little girl was fast asleep, too.

Good night!

God Watches Us

God watches o'er us all the day, at home, at school,
    and at our play;
And when the sun has left the skies, he watches
    with a million eyes.

—*Gabriel Setoun*

ood Night

Good night! Good night! Far flies the light;
But still God's love shall flame above,
Making all bright. Good night! Good night!

He prayeth well,
    Who loveth well
Both man and bird and beast.
He prayeth best,
    Who loveth best
All things both great and small;
For the dear God
    Who loveth us,
He made and loveth all.

—Samuel Taylor Coleridge,
from The Ancient Mariner

A NOTE ABOUT ELOISE WILKIN

Born in Rochester, New York, Eloise Wilkin moved with her family to New York City when she was two. One of her favorite childhood memories is of the time her mother allowed her and her brothers and sisters to scribble all over the walls of their apartment just before it was redecorated.

When she was fifteen, the family moved back to Rochester, and Ms. Wilkin studied art at the Rochester Institute of Technology before returning to New York City and embarking on her lifelong career of illustrating children's books. Most of her artwork is done in water color and a very fine line, and her books can be found in countries all around the world.

Ms. Wilkin currently lives in Rochester, where she designs doll houses and doll clothes for her many grandchildren— and, of course, continues to illustrate books for children.